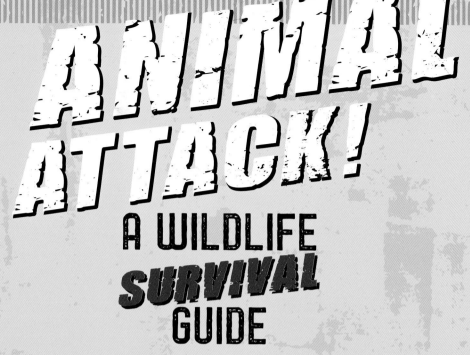

ANIMAL ATTACK!

A WILDLIFE SURVIVAL GUIDE

Written by David Rheinstrom
Designed by Nancy Panaccione & Sandra Bruner

an imprint of
SCHOLASTIC
scholastic.com

10 9 8 7 6 5 4 3 2 1
ISBN: 978-1-338-34878-1
628075 06/19
Printed in Jiaxing, China

W9-CCM-207

TABLE OF CONTENTS

Introductory Note and Legend 3

BY SEA

Tiger Shark 4
Great White Shark 8
Piranha 12
Saltwater Crocodile 16
Australian Box Jellyfish...............................20
Hippopotamus 24
Cone Snail 28
Greater Blue-Ringed Octopus 32
Stonefish 36

BY LAND

Black Mamba 40
Poison Dart Frog.......................................44
Reticulated Python 48
Gorilla..52
Cassowary 56
Grizzly Bear 60
Bengal Tiger 64
Driver Ants 68
Wild Boar 72
Wolf 76

BY AIR

Mute Swans 80
Flying Snakes 84
Tsetse Fly 88
Peregrine Falcon 92

Conclusion 96

THE WORLD IS A DANGEROUS PLACE. IT'S SWARMING WITH PERIL.

There are so many deadly critters everywhere—on land, in the seas, in the sky—that frankly, it's a wonder any of us have survived this long.

And that's where we come in. This book will teach you how to evade, outsmart, and if necessary, defeat the deadliest creatures on the planet.

But first, a word of warning:

This advice is intended for educational and joke purposes only. Please do not seek out sharks for the purpose of punching one.

Not only is that extremely foolhardy, it's also mean. Sharks gotta eat too. They're not evil. JUST HUNGRY.

GOOD LUCK OUT THERE!

LEGEND

We've developed these symbols to help you quickly identify the most important qualities of a given dangerous animal.

LARGE

VENOMOUS

FLYING

SMALL

TINY

INFECTIOUS

BITEY

BUG

CLEVER

FAST

AQUATIC

POWERFUL

SLOW

CUTE BUT DEADLY

TIGER SHARK

SCIENTIFIC NAME: *Galeocerdo cuvier*

SIZE: 10–14 ft. (3–4.25 m)

WEIGHT: 850–400 lbs. (385–635 kg)

DIET: Omnivorous

DANGER TO HUMANS: High

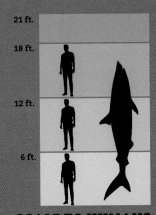

21 ft.

18 ft.

12 ft.

6 ft.

SCALE TO HUMANS

OPPONENT (GALEOCERDO CUVIER)

THE BREAKDOWN: The tops of tiger shark bodies are dark, and the bottoms of their bodies are light, making them difficult to distinguish both from above and below.

Their teeth are serrated like the edge of a knife so they are perfect for slicing through tough materials like the shells of sea turtles.

The pores near the snout are part of its *ampullae of Lorenzini*— organs that enable a shark to sense electromagnetic fields. All living things generate small amounts of electricity, so **WATCH OUT!**

NORTH AMERICA

ATLANTIC OCEAN

ASIA

AFRICA

PACIFIC OCEAN

INDIAN OCEAN

SOUTH AMERICA

AUSTRALIA

➤ WHERE IN THE WORLD?

Tiger sharks are found in warm waters all over the world: off the coasts of the Indo-Pacific, southeast and western part of Africa, on both coasts of Mexico, and beyond.

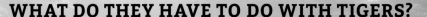

WHAT DO THEY HAVE TO DO WITH TIGERS?

Young tiger sharks have distinctive dark stripes along their sides, giving the species its name.

These stripes disappear as a tiger shark matures, but ...

ITS DANGER ONLY GROWS.

THEY'RE APEX PREDATORS, which means that in their habitats, they're at the top of the food chain, and almost never eaten by anything else. Well, *almost* anything. On very rare occasions, orcas (killer whales) have been photographed taking down and eating tiger sharks, but this is pretty uncommon.

WHAT MAKES THEM DANGEROUS? Tiger sharks are very curious and easy to provoke. On top of that, **they'll eat practically anything:** turtles, squid, birds, and lots of human garbage.

Dolphins, another frequent target, avoid areas where they know tiger sharks congregate.

SURVIVING
AN ENCOUNTER WITH A TIGER SHARK

ONE IN A MILLION—ACCORDING TO THE DEPARTMENT OF NATURAL RESOURCES IN HAWAII, THAT'S HOW LIKELY YOU ARE TO BE BITTEN BY A TIGER SHARK. IT'S A ONE-IN-A-MILLION CHANCE, **BUT JUST IN CASE ...**

1 **AVOID THE DARK.** Tiger sharks hunt at night, at dawn, and at dusk. If you're in a known shark habitat, stay out of the water at these times.

2 **PIVOT FOR PROTECTION.** Sharks ambush their prey to minimize damage to themselves; if a shark begins to circle you, follow it with your head.

3 **GO FOR THE GILLS!** Strike the shark in the side of its head with your fists, or whatever blunt object you have on hand. Try not to draw blood—you don't want to alert other sharks. You may have heard it suggested that you ought to punch it in the nose. Don't do that. Its nose is right next to its mouth.

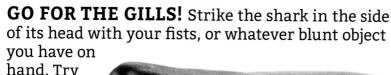

GREAT WHITE SHARK

SCIENTIFIC NAME: *Carcharodon carcharias*

SIZE: 11–16 ft. (3.3–4.9 m)

WEIGHT: 1500–4000 lbs. (680–1814 kg)

DIET: Carnivorous

DANGER TO HUMANS: Very high

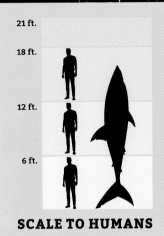

21 ft.

18 ft.

12 ft.

6 ft.

SCALE TO HUMANS

MAKING A SPLASH:
A Great White breaches
out of the water to attack.

KNOW YOUR OPPONENT

(CARCHARODON CARCHARIAS)

SHARKS DON'T BREATHE THROUGH THEIR NOSTRILS— they have gills for that. A shark's nostrils are just for smell, and they can smell very well. Sharks can analyze seawater as it flows through its nostrils using its sense organ, the ***olfactory bulb***. A Great White has the largest olfactory bulb of any shark—**18 percent of a Great White's brain is devoted to smell**. From hundreds of feet away, sharks can detect blood at a concentration of one part per million!

The first part of the Great White's scientific name, its genus, is *Carcharodon*, which comes from Greek words meaning *jagged teeth*. Look at those serrated edges! They'll cut you like butter, so watch out, buddy. Some sharks have teeth designed to hook their prey, to grab hold of it and drown it—but **Great White Shark teeth are designed to cut and sever.**

UNITED STATES

AFRICA

→ **WHERE IN THE WORLD?**
Great White Sharks are seen throughout the world's oceans, mostly in cool waters close to the coasts.

AUSTRALIA

9

THE GREAT WHITE SHARK IS ONE OF THE LARGEST PREDATORS IN THE OCEAN, and is responsible for the most unprovoked attacks on humans of any shark species.

Still, you're much more likely to be struck by lightning or hit by a bus than you are to get attacked by a shark. Despite what you may think from movies like *JAWS* or *Deep Blue Sea*, **people aren't shark food**—we don't taste great, we're not especially fatty like seals, and we've got a lot of limbs and tools for fighting back.

LET'S BE REALISTIC. If you don't go looking for shark trouble, shark trouble is unlikely to go looking for you. Great Whites are ambush hunters, so they don't like to attack groups. In other words, don't swim alone and don't swim at night. If you're bleeding, don't go in the water. But if shark trouble **does** go looking for you . . .

SURVIVING
A GREAT WHITE ATTACK

1 **BACK AWAY SLOWLY.** You want to convince the shark that you're not prey, and that you're not afraid of it. Don't splash. Stay calm. MAKE YOURSELF APPEAR AS BIG AS YOU CAN.

2 **CARRY A BIG STICK.** A blunt-ended tool called a shark billy can be used to nudge the shark away from you before it can bite. Sharks prefer easy prey, so if you can make yourself a nuisance without making it angry, you're in good shape.

3 **PUT YOURSELF IN A CORNER.** If you've got a reef or a boat or some kind of obstruction near you, put your back up against it, so the shark only has one angle of attack.

4 **EVADE THE BLADE.** If you've got a knife, **for goodness's sake DON'T USE IT.** You can't hurt a shark that badly with a knife, and even if you do draw blood, **you'll only attract more sharks.**

PIRANHA

SCIENTIFIC NAME: *Pygocentrus nattereri*

SIZE: 5–14 in. (13–35 cm)

WEIGHT: 2–8 lbs. (.9-3.6 kg)

DIET: Omnivorous

DANGER TO HUMANS: Pretty low

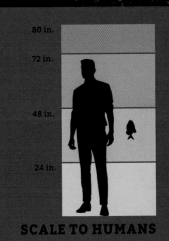

80 in.

72 in.

48 in.

24 in.

SCALE TO HUMANS

(PYGOCENTRUS NATTERERI)

THOSE PEARLY WHITES ARE PLENTY SHARP! The word piranha means tooth fish in Tupi, a native Brazilian language. Piranhas replace their teeth by section, unlike sharks, who lose and regrow individual teeth. Piranha teeth interlock with one another, ensuring a bite that clamps and tears away flesh (or fruit, or grasses, or whatever).

→ WHERE IN THE WORLD?
Piranhas are found in the Orinoco and Amazon River drainage basins in South America.

Piranhas don't just eat cows and people. They mostly eat other fish, as well as vegetation, fruits, nuts, and seeds. **Some species of piranha, in fact, are vegetarian!**

SOUTH AMERICA

THE BITES AREN'T JUST SHARP, THEY'RE POWERFUL! According to a 2012 study, the largest species of **piranha has a bite force of 72 pounds (32.7 kg)** of pressure—about half as powerful as a human bite: quite a lot for such a relatively small fish!

13

BLAME TEDDY ROOSEVELT FOR THE PIRANHA'S BAD REPUTATION.

When he traveled through Brazil in 1913, locals wanted to put on a spectacle for the visiting ex-president. So they gathered up piranhas, placed them in a netted-off stream, and starved them for several days. When Roosevelt arrived, the Brazilians hurled a cow into the stream full of ravenous fish—and soon, all that remained was a skeleton. Roosevelt wrote up the story, and soon the legend of the piranha as a bloodthirsty monster was wide-spread. Really, they're just regular, sharp-toothed fish who will probably run away from you.

The term "piranha" refers to a wide variety of freshwater fish—all of them are bony fish with powerful jaws, but none are especially dangerous to humans under normal circumstances.

AVOIDING A PIRANHA ATTACK

SCHOOLS OF PIRANHA DON'T NORMALLY ATTACK PEOPLE, ESPECIALLY IN THE WET SEASON WHEN FOOD IS ABUNDANT IN THE AMAZON. BUT WHEN IT'S DRY, THEY GET DESPERATE.

1 **DON'T BLEED IN THE WATER!** If you've got an open wound, don't try to cross a river full of piranhas. Some piranha species scavenge for food, and will seek out what they perceive to be a wounded, dying animal (that is to say, you).

2 **AVOID LITTLE PONDS IN THE DRY SEASON.** Sometimes these can be leftover pockets of water from dried-up streams or rivers, with a few very, very hungry piranhas trapped inside. Dying and desperate, **THEY MAY TRY TO CHOMP ON YOU IF YOU GET TOO CLOSE.**

3 **KEEP LITTLE KIDS OUT OF THE WATER!** Even given all the above, piranhas are still unlikely to attack a fully-grown human being. But your little sister or brother may be easy prey for a school of piranhas.

SALTWATER CROCODILE

SCIENTIFIC NAME: *Crocodylus porosus*

SIZE: 10–20 ft. (3–6 m)

WEIGHT: 880–2200 lbs. (400–1000 kg)

DIET: Carnivorous

DANGER TO HUMANS: Very, very high

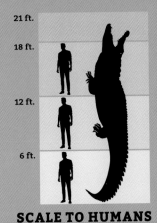

21 ft.
18 ft.
12 ft.
6 ft.

SCALE TO HUMANS

THE JAWS OF DEATH: Saltwater crocs have the world's strongest bite at **3700 pounds per square inch (psi) of force.** By contrast, human bite force is around 150-200 psi.

OPPONENT (CROCODYLUS POROSUS)

A WHALE OF A TAIL:
Saltwater crocs don't tend to move very much, which helps them conserve energy. But when they want to move, **they can launch themselves out of the water** with their powerful legs and enormous, muscled tails. As ambush hunters, they don't need to be fast for long.

INDIA

MUSCLE MOUTH: These jaws are bound up with muscles that can slam shut with incredible force, but their opening muscles aren't nearly as strong. In theory, you could hold a croc's mouth closed, but you'd still be hanging onto its neck, and it'd probably still try to throw you off and eat you.

→ WHERE IN THE WORLD?
Saltwater crocs specifically are found throughout Southeast Asia and Northern Australia.

AUSTRALIA

17

ACCORDING TO A STUDY BY THE UNIVERSITY OF FLORIDA, crocodilians (that is, crocodiles, alligators, and all their chompy cousins) **kill about 1000 people per year.** By contrast, sharks kill about 10 people per year.

Crocs are serious business, and the most serious of all is the Saltwater Crocodile, or as Australians call them, salties. They're apex predators—at the top of their food chain and proud of it—**and they'll eat absolutely anything, including you.**

THESE CREATURES ARE SMART, TERRITORIAL, AND VERY PATIENT. If they see you as food, you'd better hope you see them first—which is tough, because millions of years of evolution have shaped salties to disappear beneath the water, only their eyes and nostrils poking out of the murk.

SURVIVING
A SALTWATER CROC ATTACK

I MEAN, FIRST OF ALL, GOOD LUCK.

WHAT THE CROC WANTS TO DO IS GRAB YOU IN ITS JAWS AND PULL YOU BENEATH THE WATER TO DROWN YOU, SO IT CAN EAT YOU IN A LEISURELY MANNER ONCE YOU'RE DEAD.

SO YOU'RE GONNA NEED TO BE SMART.

RUN

1

RUN! If you see a croc, back away slowly, unless it snaps or charges. **THEN RUN!** Crocodiles can run quickly on land, but not as fast as a human, and not for very long, either. **Run in a straight line;** forget anything you heard about zig-zagging away.

2

GO FOR THE EYES. Worst-case scenario, here: the croc's clamped its jaws on you and you only have seconds to react. **GO FOR ITS EYES.** Crocodiles are bony and tough, and the only part of their faces that is even a little vulnerable is their eyes. **Sock it right in the eyeball,** and if you're very lucky, it will release you.

AUSTRALIAN BOX JELLYFISH

SCIENTIFIC NAME: *Chironex fleckeri*

SIZE: 6–9 in. (15-23 cm)

WEIGHT: 4 lbs. (1.8 kg)

DIET: Carnivorous (mostly shrimp and small fish)

DANGER TO HUMANS: Medium

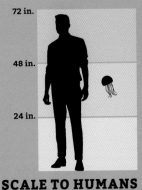

72 in.

48 in.

24 in.

SCALE TO HUMANS

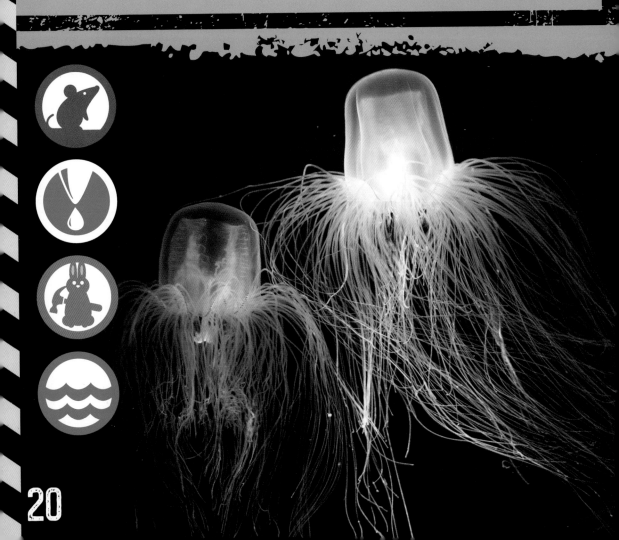

KNOW YOUR OPPONENT
(CHIRONEX FLECKERI)

AUSTRALIAN BOX JELLIES HAVE EYES—not complicated ones like a human's, but enough to distinguish light and simple shapes. This is all they need to hunt. The tentacles pull its prey into its mouth, where it is slowly digested.

Jellyfish tentacles are tipped with explosive little cells called cnidocytes (pronounced "kuh-NID-o-sites". Y'know! Just like it's spelled.).

The *cnid-* part comes from the Greek word for nettle, a kind of stinging plant—and indeed, that's how a cnidocyte behaves. When a tentacle brushes up against prey, the stinging cells trigger, and rapidly fire out little barbed points. These inject venom into the jelly's prey.

PHILIPPINES

AUSTRALIA

Box Jellyfish Safety

⚠ **DANGER**

Box Jellyfish occur in these waters. Their stings can be deadly.

Serious stings have occurred throughout the year. Take vinegar to the beach and when boating.

October – May
Jellyfish are common.
• Do not enter the water.

June – September
Jellyfish are less common but serious stings have occurred during this period.
• Be cautious if swimming and preferably wear protective clothing - especially children

First Aid

Symptoms
Immediate and increasing pain
Whitish stings adhering to skin
Red or purple weals appearing on the skin

Treatment
1. Remove victim from water
2. Monitor airway, breathing and circulation
3. Perform resuscitation if necessary
4. Flood stings with vinegar for at least 30 seconds
5. Use ice packs for pain
6. Keep victim calm and still
7. Call 000 for an Ambulance or transport to hospital

➡ WHERE IN THE WORLD?

Australian Box Jellies are mostly found in the oceans around western Australia through the northern territory and in the Indo-Pacific region.

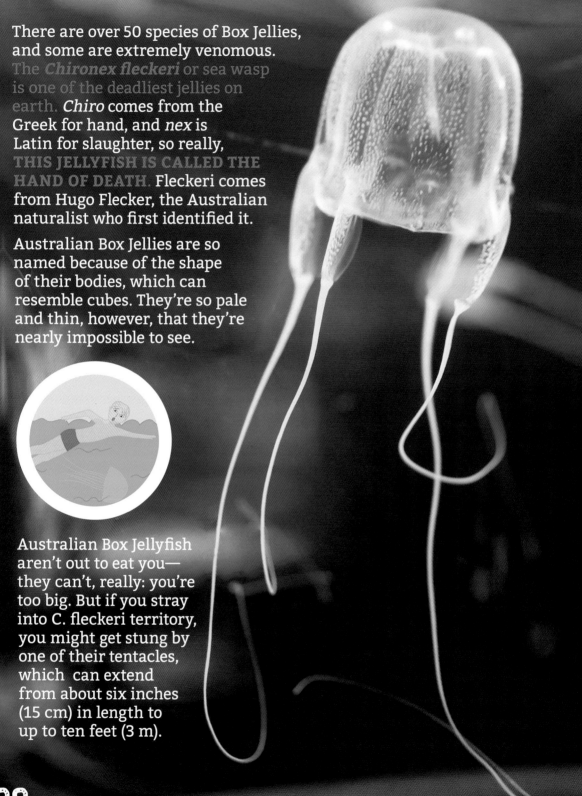

There are over 50 species of Box Jellies, and some are extremely venomous. The *Chironex fleckeri* or sea wasp is one of the deadliest jellies on earth. *Chiro* comes from the Greek for hand, and *nex* is Latin for slaughter, so really, THIS JELLYFISH IS CALLED THE HAND OF DEATH. Fleckeri comes from Hugo Flecker, the Australian naturalist who first identified it.

Australian Box Jellies are so named because of the shape of their bodies, which can resemble cubes. They're so pale and thin, however, that they're nearly impossible to see.

Australian Box Jellyfish aren't out to eat you— they can't, really: you're too big. But if you stray into C. fleckeri territory, you might get stung by one of their tentacles, which can extend from about six inches (15 cm) in length to up to ten feet (3 m).

SURVIVING
AN AUSTRALIAN BOX JELLY ATTACK

1 **MIND THE SIGN.** Most beaches in jellyfish country will post signs when too many jellies come close to shore. There are also netted beaches, with barriers strung up to prevent big beasties from coming in. However, this won't deter the thumbnail-sized, extremely dangerous Irukandji jellyfish.

STINGERS

2 **BEFRIEND A SEA TURTLE!** Sea turtles' thick skin is impervious to box jelly stings; in fact, **THEY LOVE TO EAT JELLYFISH BY THE DOZEN.** Protect yourself from jellyfish stings by donating to sea turtle conservation efforts! Beautiful ocean sunfish also subsist primarily on jellies. **HANG AROUND NEAR ONE OF THOSE, AND YOU'RE GOLDEN.**

3 **VIM AND VINEGAR.** If you get stung by a box jelly, it turns out **A LITTLE SPRAY OF VINEGAR CAN WORK WONDERS!** It prevents any unburst cnidocytes from stinging further and making anything worse. In regions where box jellies are common, you can always find spray bottles of vinegar on the beach.

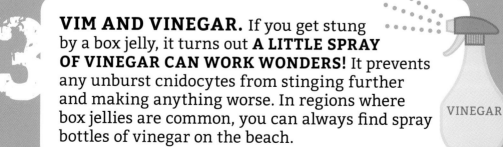

VINEGAR

HIPPOPOTAMUS

SCIENTIFIC NAME: *Hippopotamus amphibius*

SIZE: 4.9 ft. (1.5 m) tall at shoulder;
11–17 ft. (3.4–5 m) long

WEIGHT: Males - 3,310 lbs. (1501 kg)
Females - 2,870 lbs. (1301 kg)

DIET: Herbivorous

DANGER TO HUMANS: High

18 ft.
12 ft.
6 ft.

SCALE TO HUMANS

OPEN WIDE:
A hippopotamus's jaws can hinge open nearly 180 degrees. That'd be like opening up your own mouth and folding it open like a book. Like this book. Please do not attempt this at home.

KNOW YOUR
OPPONENT
(HIPPOPOTAMUS AMPHIBIUS)

BLOOD, SWEAT, AND TEARS: Actually, it's none of those. Hippos secrete an acidic, reddish-brown fluid that works as a kind of natural sunscreen and antibacterial agent. **Hippos have very thick skin** (2 in./5 cm thick!), but they also fight and gouge each other a lot with their sharp teeth. It helps to have your own house-made antibacterial spray in cases like that.

NILE DELTA

AFRICA

➡ WHERE IN THE WORLD?
Hippos are found near the Nile delta and sub-Saharan Africa.

THIS ONE'S A LITTLE GROSS: Hippos are extremely territorial, and they use their **feces** (their poop) to mark that territory. When they do their marking, they—well, there's no polite way to say this—they spin their tails, spraying droppings as far and wide as possible. In other words, NEVER STAND BEHIND A HIPPO.

THE NAME HIPPOPOTAMUS COMES FROM GREEK: hippo means horse; potamus means from the river. They're water horses, or at least in name, but hippos are more closely related to whales, dolphins, and orcas than they are to horses.

They only eat grasses in the wild, so what's with the huge, predatory-looking canines? THE SHORT ANSWER IS: HIPPOS ARE MEAN.

They use their big, sharp teeth to battle for dominance within their own pods—and to fend off those predators foolish enough to think they could snatch a baby hippo.

HIPPOS SPEND MOST OF THEIR LIVES IN THE WATER: to keep cool during the long, hot sub-Saharan days, they stay submerged while the sun is out, coming out of the water to graze when the sun sets.

HIPPOS EVEN SLEEP UNDERWATER: they come out of the water to breathe subconsciously—it happens automatically without waking up or needing to think about it.

SURVIVING
A HIPPO ATTACK

SO HIPPOS ARE HERBIVORES. THE ONLY REASON A HIPPO WILL ASSAULT YOU IS IF YOU'VE INTRUDED ON ITS TERRITORY AND SURPRISED IT.

1

IF THEY YAWN, GET GONE! That hippo isn't tired, he's challenging you. Bull hippos show their teeth when they're threatened, and if you can see them, then an attack is imminent. **Get out of the way NOW.**

2

IF YOU'RE IN THE WATER AND SEE A HIPPO IN THE DISTANCE, make your presence known, especially if you see hippos submerging. Make a lot of noise, generate a lot of bubbles—and GET OUT OF THE AREA AS QUICKLY AS YOU CAN.

3

BE AWARE! Watch for hippo poop on the ground. If you see it, and it's fresh, steer clear.

4

HEAD FOR THE HILLS. Hippos may look tubby and slow, but they can run about as fast as humans can for short distances. If you are chased by a hippo, don't run in a straight line—**head for the trees, run around a rocky outcrop, or jump over an anthill.**

27

CONE SNAIL

SCIENTIFIC NAME: *Conidae*

SIZE: Varied (up to 9 in./23 cm long)

WEIGHT: Up to 3.5 oz. (100 g)

DIET: Carnivorous (marine worms, small fish and mollusks, other cone snails)

DANGER TO HUMANS: High (non-aggressive, but extremely toxic)

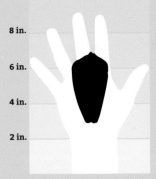

8 in.

6 in.

4 in.

2 in.

SCALE TO HUMANS

KNOW YOUR
OPPONENT (CONIDAE)

TOOTH OR DARE:
The barbed tooth-like body part that a cone snail uses to poison its prey is called a radula—it's something common to most mollusks, though most are just barbed tongues, not poison darts. When a cone snail senses prey, it extends its little poison tooth on a proboscis—a long, fleshy protrusion—and harpoons it! The venom paralyzes the prey, and the proboscis retracts, dragging the food into the snail's mouth.

LOVELY BUT LETHAL: The gorgeous shell of a textile cone makes it extremely tempting and dangerous to human divers. The shell itself isn't dangerous, but **THE SNAIL INSIDE IS EXTREMELY VENOMOUS.**

UNITED STATES

➤ WHERE IN THE WORLD?

There are over 800 different species of cone snails that are found in warm tropical seas and oceans worldwide.

AFRICA

SOUTH
AMERICA

AUSTRALIA

Cone snails are a family of predatory mollusks with over 800 species. Not all of them are dangerous to humans, but some, especially the textile and the geography cone, are fatally venomous. In fact, conotoxin is arguably the most concentrated venom on the planet.

ONE CONE SNAIL HAS ENOUGH VENOM TO POTENTIALLY KILL UP TO 700 PEOPLE.

Interestingly, the different neurotoxins from cone snails are being studied by scientists to see if they can take some of the less poisonous bits and make them into medicines that treat depression and seizures, among other ailments.

The different species of cone snail all eat different things: other snails, sea worms, and little fish. Notice: none of those things are human beings. Among the smaller cone snails, especially the ones that hunt worms, the toxins are less potent, and hurt about as much as a bee-sting (which is to say, they still hurt!).

SURVIVING
A CONE SNAIL ENCOUNTER

THIS IS VERY EASY. DON'T TOUCH IT!

A CONE SNAIL'S RADULA CAN PUNCH THROUGH YOUR THICK GLOVES, or your wetsuit, or your flippers. Some of these things eat other snails; you think a half-centimeter of rubber will stop a poison-tipped harpoon?

DON'T TOUCH!!

GREATER BLUE-RINGED OCTOPUS

SCIENTIFIC NAME: *Hapalochlaena Lunulata*

SIZE: 4 in. (10 cm)

WEIGHT: 3 oz. (80 g)

DIET: Carnivorous (mostly crustaceans)

DANGER TO HUMANS: Low - Medium

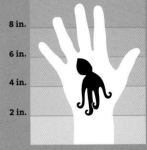

8 in.
6 in.
4 in.
2 in.

SCALE TO HUMANS

LE BEAK, C'EST CHIC: this is the danger zone, right here. The greater blue-ringed octopus's saliva has venoms in it that **PARALYZE YOUR LIMBS AND HALT ORGANS.**

(HAPALOCHLAENA LUNULATA)

A GREATER BLUE-RINGED OCTOPUS IS ONLY ABOUT 4 INCHES (10 cm) LONG FROM MANTLE TO TENTACLE. IT'S VERY CUTE, UNFORTUNATELY.

JAPAN

THE RING'S THE THING:
They're beautiful, right? Well, you're meant to notice them. They're a signal to predators that says, **"Hey! I'm venomous! Don't eat me!"** Remember, the greater blue-ringed octopus is teensy-tiny. They call it greater because of the size of its rings.

AUSTRALIA

➡ WHERE IN THE WORLD?
Greater blue-ringed octopuses are found from Northern Australia to Japan, including Papua New Guinea, Solomon Islands, and Indonesia as far west as Sri Lanka.

SALIVA VENOMS:
One of those venoms is a deadly tetrodotoxin, which is similar to the kinds of venom you might find in a pufferfish. Tetrodotoxin interferes with your nervous system, causing your body to lock up. A greater blue-ringed octopus bite makes the affected area go numb. Then, you'll throw up and have trouble breathing, and maybe even have a fatal heart attack. DON'T MESS WITH THEM!

33

Octopuses like the greater blue-ringed one live solitary lives, hunting down crabs and cockles in warm tropical waters. They live in little burrows or dens, dragging their kills back home to nibble upon.

OCTOPUSES AREN'T GENERALLY AGGRESSIVE—and, in fact, when it's not threatened, the greater blue-ringed octopus doesn't appear that blue at all! **The rings show up when the octopus is freaked out**—it uses light-reflecting cells called iridophores and color-changing cells called chromatophors to show off and highlight their blue rings. Normally, these octopuses look sort of beige-y to brown.

IF YOU SEE BLUE: you've scared it, and that means it might bite you, so **STAY BACK!**

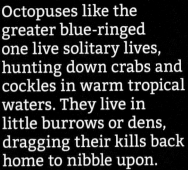

SURVIVING
A GREATER BLUE-RINGED OCTOPUS ATTACK

IF YOU'RE FOOLISH ENOUGH TO BOTHER A GREATER BLUE-RINGED OCTOPUS, AND UNLUCKY ENOUGH TO RECEIVE A BITE FROM ONE, DO THE FOLLOWING:

1

GET OUT OF THE WATER. The effects of tetrodotoxin can take hold in **under five minutes.**

5 min

GET OUT!!

CONTINUOUS
CPR

2

GET A FRIEND. You're going to lose control of your body very soon, so you're going to need help getting to a hospital. If things go very badly, your friend will need to **perform CPR continuously** until paramedics arrive to put you on a ventilator. Remember, tetrodotoxin takes away your ability to breathe unassisted, but keeps you awake and conscious throughout the whole ordeal. **IT'S HORRIFYING!**

3

GET TO THE HOSPITAL.
If you can get yourself put on an artificial respirator, you're **going to live**. Despite its terrifying effects, the tetrodotoxin doesn't last more than a day. **Your body will flush the toxin and you will regain the ability to breathe.**

STONEFISH

SCIENTIFIC NAME: *Synancelidae*

SIZE: 14–20 in. (35–50 cm)

WEIGHT: up to 5 lbs. (2.3 kg)

DIET: Carnivorous (mostly fish and crustaceans)

DANGER TO HUMANS: Medium

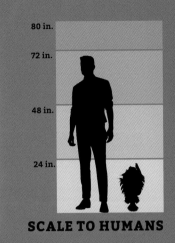

80 in.

72 in.

48 in.

24 in.

SCALE TO HUMANS

Stonefish can survive for up to a day out of water, and if they wash ashore, they can blend in easily with craggy rocks.

SPINE YOUR OWN BUSINESS:

These dorsal (back) spines are filled with a powerful neurotoxin, but almost as nasty as the venom are the spines themselves—**they're long, sharp, and tough, and can pierce through the sole of a shoe.**

WHERE IN THE WORLD?

Stonefish are found in the Indian and Pacific Oceans, extending to northern Australia.

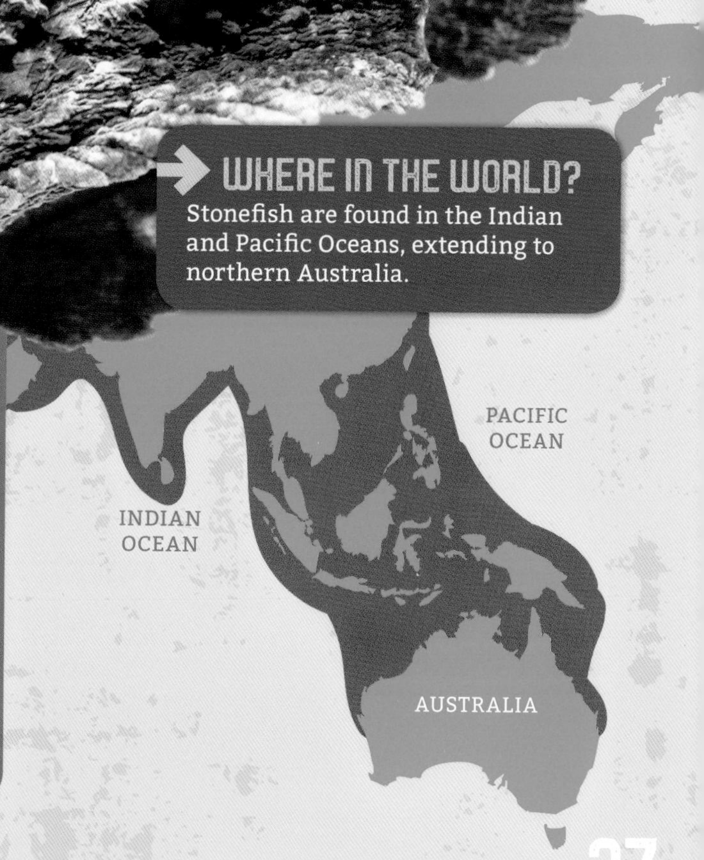

NOW YOU SEE ME: Stonefish are hunters that prey on smaller fish and crustaceans. They lie in wait amid brightly-colored coral reefs or brownish-grey stones covered in weeds—this deceptive camouflage is what gives the stonefish its name.

PACIFIC OCEAN

INDIAN OCEAN

AUSTRALIA

37

STONEFISH DON'T WANT TO EAT YOU.
You're too big. But they also don't want to be attacked by you, which is why they have the spines and the venom. Sometimes, they travel well beyond the warm coastal reef waters and into tidal pools—or they may be stranded by the tide on a beach.

THE SPINES ARE SERIOUS BUSINESS.
There is a case of a man in Western Australia whose thick-soled boot was punctured by a stonefish spine. When the spine punctures the skin, venom sacs at the base of the spine deploy, squirting toxins deep into the wound.

SURVIVING
A STONEFISH ATTACK

GETTING STUNG BY A STONEFISH IS EXCRUCIATINGLY PAINFUL. NOT ONLY DOES IT BURN AND STING, BUT THERE'S ALSO THIS GREAT BIG NEEDLE OF A SPINE THAT PUNCTURES YOUR FOOT. IT'S NO GOOD!

LEFT UNTREATED, A STONEFISH STING CAN RESULT IN TISSUE NECROSIS (ROT) AND EVEN DEATH.

FORTUNATELY, THERE'S ANTIVENOM!

1 TAKE YOUR MEDICINE! Antivenom treatments are available for stonefish—these help to reduce the swelling and the deadly effect of the toxin.

1 hr

2 TAKE A BATH! Hot water (113 degrees F/45 C) degrades the proteins in stonefish toxin, so if you're injured by one, **IMMERSE THE AFFECTED AREA IN HOT WATER FOR AN HOUR**. Studies have proven that hot water, together with antivenom and pain medication, can fend off the worst effects of a stonefish wound.

113°

BLACK MAMBA

SCIENTIFIC NAME: *Dendroaspis Polylepsis*

SIZE: 6.6–9.8 ft. (2–3 m)

WEIGHT: 3.5 lbs. (1.6 kg)

DIET: Carnivorous

DANGER TO HUMANS: High

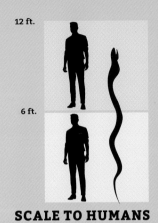

12 ft.

6 ft.

SCALE TO HUMANS

STRIKE A POSE:
The mamba lifts its head and appears to be smiling, but don't let this cute face fool you. Mambas are deadly to humans, so **KEEP YOUR DISTANCE.**

OPPONENT

(DENDROASPIS POLYLEPSIS)

PARTY IN THE FRONT:

The black mamba has fangs in the front of its mouth, and few other teeth in its upper jaw—this kind of mouth is specific to elapids, the family of venomous snakes that includes mambas, cobras, and coral snakes. **This dental arrangement allows the mamba to inject venom quickly with multiple strikes.**

BUSINESS IN THE BACK:

Black mambas are the longest venomous snakes in Africa, and they're also the fastest. A full-grown black mamba can be almost 10 feet (3 m) long, and it can lift up more of its upper body than most snakes, so in addition to being able to hustle along at about 12 miles per hour (19 kph), it can launch its upper body at tall prey from surprising distances.

12 mph (19 kph)

AFRICA

→ WHERE IN THE WORLD?

Black mambas are found in the Horn of Africa and parts of the southeast.

BLACK MAMBAS ARE SOME OF THE DEADLIEST SNAKES ON THE PLANET. A bite can kill an adult human in a matter of hours, though antivenoms have been developed to treat the poison. These snakes primarily eat little fuzzy critters like bats and bush babies, darting out from cover to strike, incapacitate, and swallow their prey.

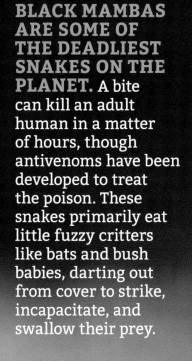

Mamba comes from the Zulu word for the animal, imamba. You'll notice, looking at the snake, that it's not really black—not on the outside, anyway. Its scales are usually grayish-brown. However, the inside of its terrifying mouth is black, giving it the name.

FULL-GROWN BLACK MAMBAS HAVE ONLY A HANDFUL OF PREDATORS: Snake-eating birds of prey, which can crush or immobilize the snake's head with their claws, and the Cape file snake, which has a natural immunity to snake venom. Younger mambas are vulnerable to mongooses, speedy mammals with a similar (though limited) resistance to venom.

SURVIVING
A BLACK MAMBA ATTACK

MAMBAS ARE VERY EASY TO STARTLE AND WILL ATTACK YOU IF THEY'RE FRIGHTENED. REMEMBER, THEY MAY BE LONG, BUT THEY'RE STILL MUCH SMALLER THAN YOU.

HISS

1 **WATCH FOR THE HOOD, LISTEN FOR THE HISS.** First of all, if you do see a black mamba, just back away slowly. Don't make sudden movements; it'll freak out the snake. **Mambas have hoods like cobras do, but they're smaller**. A threatened black mamba will rear up, flare its hood, open its mouth and flick its tongue, and hiss at you. **DON'T ENGAGE IT. MOVE AWAY.**

2 **APPLY A TOURNIQUET.** If you receive a bite, you want to prevent that venom from spreading. Wrap an area above the wound (closer to your heart) with fabric; wrap a loop around a stick and twist until the fabric becomes very tight. It's gonna hurt, but it might just save your life by preventing the venom from reaching your heart. This advice is only for mamba venom, because the neurotoxin is a greater risk than possible tissue necrosis from the tourniquet. For other snakes with different venoms, avoid tourniquets.

3 **THEY HAVE ANTIVENOM NOW.** Go to the hospital. Get treatment. **Don't try to be tough** and say you don't need it; get the antivenom so you don't die of a heart attack four hours from now.

POISON DART FROG

SCIENTIFIC NAME: *Dendrobatidae*

SIZE: 1–1.5 in. (2.5–4 cm)

WEIGHT: 1 oz. (28 g)

DIET: Insectivorous

DANGER TO HUMANS: Low, unless you eat one.

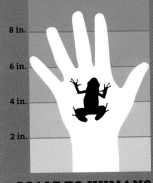

8 in.
6 in.
4 in.
2 in.

SCALE TO HUMANS

OPPONENT (DENDROBATIDAE)

PURE POISON!

The skin of a poison dart frog is coated with a layer of chemicals called alkaloids, which in this case are extremely toxic. All alkaloids aren't necessarily poisons; for example, caffeine is an alkaloid. That said, don't put a frog in your coffee.

SIGN SAYS: STAY AWAY, FOOLS!

The distinctive bright colors and markings of a poison dart frog are a type of biological warning marker called aposematism (which is a shorter, more technical term for a sign on an animal or a plant that tells you to go away). These frogs are pretty small, and would make easy prey for a larger predator.

Amazon River basin

SOUTH AMERICA

➡ WHERE IN THE WORLD?

Poison dart frogs are found throughout most of northern South America—anywhere within the drainage basin of the Amazon, and about as far south as Brazil's border with Argentina.

These little creatures are called poison dart frogs because of the toxins they secrete from their skins. Indigenous people of South America have used these toxins to tip the darts they use for hunting for thousands of years.

IT'S THE FROG'S NATIVE DIET THAT MAKES THEM SO TOXIC: Poison dart frogs in the wild eat a great deal of ants, especially those ants with powerful and painful stings. In order to metabolize these poisons, the frog's body expels them through the skin. It's like how if you, a human, eat a bunch of garlic, your sweat will smell like garlic for the next twelve hours or so. **Like that, but with poison. Y'know, relatable!**

The point is that in captivity, fed a diet of non-poisonous insects, poison dart frogs don't secrete any poison. But with their wild diets, collecting all those toxins, they're some of the most dangerous animals on the South American continent.

SURVIVING
A POISON DART FROG ENCOUNTER

THIS ONE'S RELATIVELY EASY. IF SEEN IN THE WILD, DON'T TOUCH ONE. ADMIRE ITS BEAUTY FROM A DISTANCE.

CAPTURE IT WITH YOUR CAMERA, NOT YOUR HANDS.

AUTO   00:07:14

3...2...1...I...1...2...3

MIGHT POISON CURE POISON?

There's no known antidote for batrachotoxin, one of the main alkaloid toxins found in poison dart frogs, but the way they work can provide some clues. The toxin results in body paralysis by opening up the sodium channels in your neurons. This works precisely the opposite way from tetrodotoxin, the sodium blocker found in the greater blue-ringed octopus. So it's a possibility that the two incredibly powerful toxins cancel each other out. I'm not interested in finding out whether or not it works.

RETICULATED PYTHON

SCIENTIFIC NAME: *Python reticulatus*

SIZE: 10–21 ft. (3–6.5 m) long

WEIGHT: 165–250 lbs. (75–113 kg)

DIET: Carnivorous

DANGER TO HUMANS: High

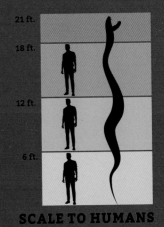

21 ft.
18 ft.
12 ft.
6 ft.

SCALE TO HUMANS

WIGGLE IN THE WATER: Reticulated pythons are powerful swimmers and move through the water as swiftly as they move on land. They can swim, submerged, for half an hour before surfacing to breathe. This has enabled the reticulated python to island-hop from its original home in continental Southeast Asia to the island countries of the Malay Archipelago, and beyond.

OPPONENT
(PYTHON RETICULATUS)

A TIGHT SPOT: The reticulated python is a constrictor—it wraps its coils around its prey. This cuts off blood flow to internal organs; the prey animal loses consciousness and dies. This can take minutes or even seconds.

OPEN REAL WIDE:

A python swallows its prey whole, digesting it slowly over a number of weeks or even months. The reticulated python is one of the few constrictor snakes large enough to swallow a full-grown human being.

INDIA

→ WHERE IN THE WORLD?

Reticulated Pythons are found from India to Indonesia.

INDONESIA

The reticulated python is the world's longest snake and among the heaviest. Its name comes from the Latin word rete (compare to the Great White Shark's rete mirabile, the wonderful net), because of the net-like patterns of its coloration. They're not venomous, but they don't need to be. With their steely, well-muscled bulk, they can coil and kill pretty much any medium-sized mammal.

Humans are at around the upper range of its prey weight—pythons usually can't eat anything that weighs more than they do, so big creatures like full-grown tigers or water buffalo are safe. It's people, up to about 170 pounds (73 kg) or so, that are vulnerable.

SURVIVING
A RETICULATED PYTHON ATTACK

1 **KNIFE TO MEET YOU.** If you're in an area known for being infested with pythons, carry a small blade. Better yet, carry it on a lanyard wrapped around your wrist. **If a python attacks and starts to constrict, start stabbing.** You're unlikely to kill the thing, but you'll wound it badly enough to convince it you're not worth the trouble.

Rubbing Alcohol

2 **SPRAY IT, DON'T SAY IT.** Some wilderness explorers carry little spray bottles of rubbing alcohol in case they encounter pythons, to spray into their eyes and mouth. The foreign, burning sensation startles and bothers the snake, sometimes frightening it away.

3 **IT'S A WRAP.** The thing to keep in mind here is that you **cannot let it wrap around you**. Once you're constricted, it's over. **Surviving a python attack means preventing constriction at all costs.**

GORILLA

SCIENTIFIC NAME: *Gorilla gorilla*

SIZE: 5.2 ft. (1.6 m)

WEIGHT: 150–430 lbs. (68–195 kg)

DIET: Herbivorous

DANGER TO HUMANS: Low

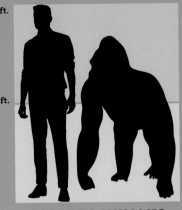

6 ft.

3 ft.

SCALE TO HUMANS

GORILLAS WALK ON THEIR KNUCKLES, but can walk on two feet like humans when necessary. Gorillas also stand upright when making defensive displays.

52

(GORILLA GORILLA)

AFRICA

CREST IS BEST:

The protrusion on an adult male gorilla's skull is called the sagittal crest. It's an anchor point for powerful chewing muscles, which the gorilla needs to munch through its diet of fibrous leaves and shoots.

➡ WHERE IN THE WORLD?

Gorillas are found in eastern Democratic Republic of Congo (DRC), Uganda, and Rwanda, while mountain gorillas are only found within the Virunga mountain region straddling the DRC, Rwanda, and Uganda borders.

THE GLINT OF SILVER:

Mature male mountain gorillas go grey in a very specific way: on their backs. If you see a silverback gorilla, you'll probably see the rest of his troop soon. Silverbacks are the heads of their families and protect them fiercely.

53

GORILLAS ARE EXTREMELY SMART.

They're some of our closest living relatives—and gorillas in captivity have learned to communicate with humans using sign language. Gorillas live into their late 40s, generally, if they aren't killed by disease or human poachers.

Gorillas are critically endangered, and, as it stands, humans pose significantly more of a threat to them than they do to us. Gorillas are frightened of people, and have a vegetarian diet. If you find yourself fighting a gorilla, I'm sorry, but it was probably YOUR fault.

SO IF THEY'RE SO PEACEFUL AND SMART, WHY DO THEY HAVE SUCH GREAT BIG CANINES? Male gorillas battle one another for dominance of their troops, and inflict bites on one another. However, combat-by-biting is usually the last and rarest step of a ritualized dominance display. If hooting, tossing leaves, standing erect, beating the chest, and charging doesn't intimidate a rival, then the combat commences.

SURVIVING
A GORILLA ATTACK

GORILLAS ARE EXTREMELY POWERFUL ANIMALS WITH IMMENSE PHYSICAL STRENGTH AND AGILITY. YOU WILL NOT BE ABLE TO OUT-WRESTLE, OUT-MANEUVER, OR OUT-THINK A FULL-GROWN MOUNTAIN GORILLA. **THE KEY IS TO DE-ESCALATE.**

THE GORILLA DOESN'T WANT TO HAVE TO HURT YOU; YOU JUST NEED TO PROVE YOU'RE NOT A THREAT TO HIM.

CROUCH DOWN!

1 LET'S GET SMALL. You're a primate; he's a primate. There's a chance the gorilla interprets your presence as a threat to his troop or territory. Crouch down and ball yourself up so you look tiny and harmless.

2 DON'T SMILE. Baring teeth is one of the ways that great apes communicate anger and aggression. Keep your mouth shut, lest the gorilla think you're issuing a challenge.

3 AVOID EYE CONTACT. Another way that gorillas signal a challenge is through direct, confrontational eye contact. Do not engage the gorilla; **LOOK DOWN, ACT TIMID, AND SLOWLY BACK AWAY.**

CASSOWARY

SCIENTIFIC NAME: *Casuarius casuarius*

SIZE: 5–6 ft. (1.5–1.8 m)

WEIGHT: 75–128 lbs. (34–58 kg)

DIET: Omnivorous

DANGER TO HUMANS: Medium

6 ft.

3 ft.

SCALE TO HUMANS

KNOW YOUR OPPONENT

(STRUTHIO CASUARIUS)

THIS CREST ATOP THE CASSOWARY'S HEAD IS CALLED A CASQUE, whose purpose is not entirely known. It may be the case that, similar to the cranial chambers of their dinosaur ancestors, **the casque is a resonant chamber to amplify cassowary mating calls.** It may also function as a secondary sex characteristic, demonstrating attractiveness and fitness to other cassowaries.

THE CLAW: Cassowaries eat exclusively fruit, so they don't use their enormous claws to hunt. Instead, **this is a defensive weapon.** The innermost toe of their three-toed foot (like the big toe on a human foot) has a very large, elongated claw.

THIS DANGLY BIT IS CALLED THE WATTLE; many bird species have them—**you might be most familiar with the wattle of a rooster or turkey.** These function as a fancy display for the cassowaries, which show them off to potential mates.

WHERE IN THE WORLD? Cassowaries are found in New Guinea and Australia.

NEW GUINEA

AUSTRALIA

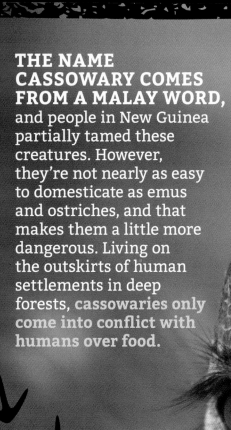

THE NAME CASSOWARY COMES FROM A MALAY WORD, and people in New Guinea partially tamed these creatures. However, they're not nearly as easy to domesticate as emus and ostriches, and that makes them a little more dangerous. Living on the outskirts of human settlements in deep forests, cassowaries only come into conflict with humans over food.

Toying with, teasing, or feeding wild cassowaries is what usually results in attacks.

30mph
(48 kph)

CASSOWARIES ARE LIVING RELICS.

Paleontologists suggest that many dinosaurs had a look similar to cassowaries. They're flightless birds, but they make up for this lack of aviation with startling speed: their powerful legs can propel them along the ground at over 30 miles per hour (48 kph). They're some of the largest birds in the world, smaller only than the emu and the ostrich.

SURVIVING
A CASSOWARY ATTACK

1

KEEP YOUR DOG INSIDE.
Dingoes and wild dogs are some of the cassowary's only natural enemies. This means that if you're traveling with a dog, and you see a cassowary, GRAB IT AND RUN. **The cassowary will attack without provocation.**

2

STAY ON YOUR FEET.
A cassowary isn't going to try to kill you on purpose. It wants to wound you so you don't follow it back into the woods. STAY UPRIGHT, because if you fall, there's a possibility that the slashing claw of the cassowary will cut open your neck.

3

KEEP DRIVING. Cassowaries have come to associate humans (and cars) with food. Cassowaries also don't like reflective surfaces like windows, because sometimes they think there's another cassowary looking back at them.
THEY'RE MEAN, NOT SMART.
Do not get out of the car to shoo it off.
DRIVE AWAY. DRIVE FAST. KEEP GOING.

30 MPH
(48 kph)

GRIZZLY BEAR

SCIENTIFIC NAME: *Ursus arctos*

SIZE: 6–9 ft. (2.7–4 m) high on hind legs, 3–5 ft. (1.4–2.3 m) high at the shoulder

WEIGHT: Males 300–600 lbs. (136–272 kg), females 200–400 lbs. (91–181 kg)

DIET: Omnivorous

DANGER TO HUMANS: High

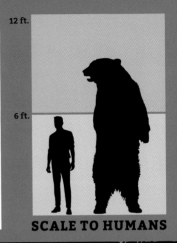

12 ft.

6 ft.

SCALE TO HUMANS

OPPONENT (URSUS ARCTOS)

According to the National Park Service, **BEARS HAVE THE KEENEST SENSE OF SMELL IN THE ANIMAL KINGDOM**, better even than a dog's. They can smell fresh kills made by other predators many miles away, and rush in to scavenge the kill.

> ## WHERE IN THE WORLD?
> Grizzly bears are found in many different habitats, from dense forests to subalpine meadows, open plains and arctic tundra in North America.

NORTH AMERICA

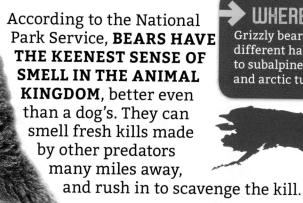

Grizzlies use their claws to dig for roots or clams, trap fish, and pummel and gore enemies.

A GRIZZLY HAS A DISTINCTIVE 'HUMP' ON ITS SHOULDERS, which is useful only to humans in distinguishing them from black bears, which are less dangerous and easier to frighten away.

GRIZZLIES ARE LARGE, OMNIVOROUS BEARS THAT PREY ON THE LARGEST ANIMALS IN THE NORTH AMERICAN CONTINENT: bison, elk, and moose. They also fish for salmon and trout, forage for berries, and eat little mammals too, like rats and voles.

Bears are smart, and they've learned that humans can be very loud and dangerous. *BUT* **a very hungry, very determined bear may maul you, SO IT'S IMPORTANT TO KEEP A COOL HEAD.**

SURVIVING
A GRIZZLY ATTACK

FIRST THINGS FIRST: STAY CALM, AND IDENTIFY THE BEAR'S ATTITUDE. THERE ARE TWO DIFFERENT APPROACHES YOU'LL WANT TO TAKE, DEPENDING ON WHETHER OR NOT THE BEAR IS BEING DEFENSIVE OR PREDATORY.

1

DEALING WITH A DEFENSIVE GRIZZLY BEAR. REMAIN CALM. Slowly wave your hands over your head and talk to the bear—it won't understand you, but you'll help it realize that you mean it no harm. If the bear approaches, lie on your stomach, and interlock your hands behind your neck. The bear will try to turn you over because it's curious. Roll back onto your belly. Eventually, the bear will determine you're not a threat and leave you be.

SIGNS OF DEFENSIVENESS:
The bear makes a lot of noise.
Its cubs are around.
It paws at the ground.

2

SIGNS OF AGITATION:
It sways its head, huffs, pops its jaws, snorts, or clacks its teeth. Lowered head and laid-back ears also indicate aggression.

DEALING WITH A PREDATORY BEAR. If it engages, **FIGHT FOR YOUR LIFE.** Go for its eyes with whatever you've got at hand: rocks, your thermos, bear spray; whatever. If you've got a gun, don't bother—you won't kill it, you'll just make it angrier.

63

BENGAL TIGER

SCIENTIFIC NAME: *Panthera tigris tigris*

SIZE: 8.7–10 ft. (2.6–3 m)

WEIGHT: 220–569 lbs. (100–258 kg)

DIET: Carnivorous

DANGER TO HUMANS: Very high

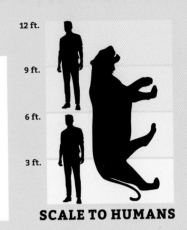

12 ft.
9 ft.
6 ft.
3 ft.

SCALE TO HUMANS

TIGERS HAVE THE LARGEST TEETH IN THE ANIMAL KINGDOM: Their canines can reach up to **4 inches (10 cm)** in length!

KNOW YOUR
OPPONENT
(PANTHERA TIGRIS TIGRIS)

A TIGER IS STRIPED FOR CAMOUFLAGE PURPOSES — it's an ambush hunter and likes to conceal itself in dense foliage.

A prey animal might mistake its black and orange striping for the play of shadow over some tall grass.

INDIA

➤ **WHERE IN THE WORLD?**
Bengal tigers are in scattered regions throughout India, Bangladesh, Myanmar, Nepal, and Bhutan.

The national symbols of both India and Bangladesh, the **BENGAL TIGER IS ONE OF THE DEADLIEST ANIMALS IN THE WORLD**—especially to humans. Ecology researchers at Colby College in Maine compared the most accurate reports they could find and determined that **between 1800 and 2009, tigers killed about 373,000 human beings,** which is slightly less than the population of New Orleans, Louisiana.

THAT IS A LOT OF PEOPLE.

TIGERS DO NOT MESS AROUND.

TIGERS ARE EXPERT HUNTERS. They are patient and smart, and they eat antelope-like creatures as the main component of their diet. **However, this hasn't stopped some of them for developing a taste for human meat.** Man-eating tigers have terrorized rural towns in Southeast Asia for centuries—perhaps the most notable one, the Champawat Tiger, killed an estimated 436 people before a hunter, brought to the village of Champawat for this very purpose, shot her dead in 1907.

SURVIVING
A BENGEL TIGER ATTACK

THERE ARE A LOT OF THINGS THAT WON'T WORK, FIRST OF ALL. PUTTING A MASK ON THE BACK OF YOUR HEAD SO THE TIGER THINKS YOU'RE STILL FACING IT DOESN'T WORK. PLAYING DEAD DEFINITELY DOESN'T WORK.

1

FACE IT DOWN. But don't make eye contact. Back away slowly; you don't want to make the tiger think it's got an opportunity to chase you. **They love chases.**

2

MAKE SOME NOISE. Unexpected noises will freak out and possibly scare off the tiger. Yell as loud as you can. Jingle your keys! Play loud music on your phone. Seriously, anything piercing or weird might just do the trick; now's the time to try out that scream-based performance art piece you've been considering.

ROCK -N- ROLL

DRIVER ANTS

SCIENTIFIC NAME: *Dorylus* Genus

SIZE: 0.1 in. (7.5 mm)

WEIGHT: .00017 oz. (5 mg)

DIET: Insectivous, but will occasionally eat mammals

DANGER TO HUMANS: Low

8 in.

6 in.

4 in.

2 in.

SCALE TO HUMANS

AFRICA

SOLDIER ANTS:
Big and mean, with huge mandibles (jaws), these enormous females protect the column as it moves along.

➡ **WHERE IN THE WORLD?**
Dorylus genus are found in Africa.

WORKER ANT:
By far the largest proportion of ants in the nest, these sterile females travel and forage. Note their very large mandibles!

QUEEN ANT: One per colony. Lays millions of eggs. Stays in the nest.

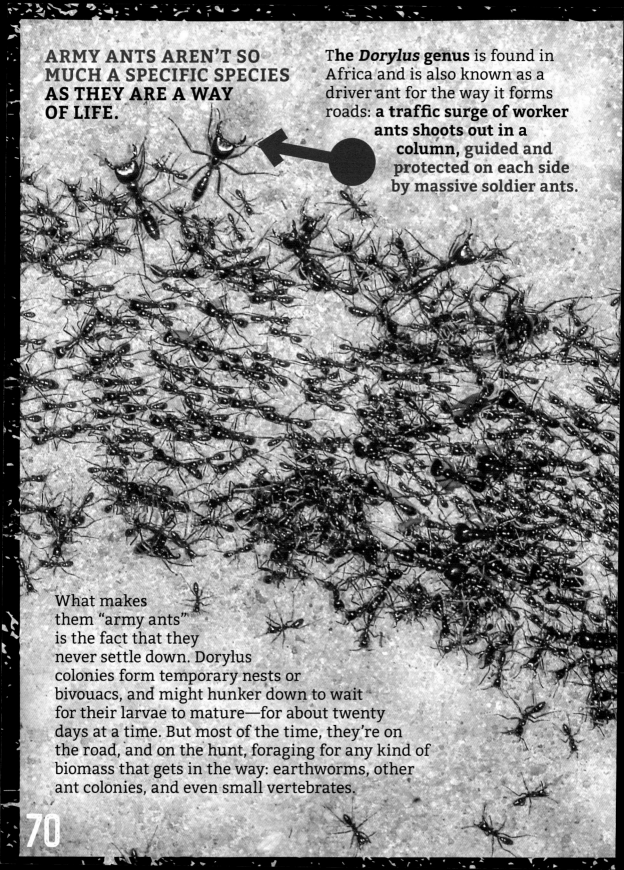

ARMY ANTS AREN'T SO MUCH A SPECIFIC SPECIES AS THEY ARE A WAY OF LIFE.

The *Dorylus* genus is found in Africa and is also known as a driver ant for the way it forms roads: **a traffic surge of worker ants shoots out in a column,** guided and protected on each side by massive soldier ants.

What makes them "army ants" is the fact that they never settle down. Dorylus colonies form temporary nests or bivouacs, and might hunker down to wait for their larvae to mature—for about twenty days at a time. But most of the time, they're on the road, and on the hunt, foraging for any kind of biomass that gets in the way: earthworms, other ant colonies, and even small vertebrates.

SURVIVING
A DRIVER ANT ATTACK

LET'S GET REAL HERE: YOU'RE A HUMAN; THEY'RE ANTS. THEY'RE NOT GOING TO SWARM UP YOUR BODY AS YOU WALK AND TAKE YOU DOWN, BUT YOU DEFINITELY DON'T WANT TO WALK RIGHT THROUGH THE MIDDLE OF A DRIVER ANT COLUMN, WHICH CAN BE OVER 300 FEET (91 M) LONG.

WE'RE LUCKY, IN A WAY. Despite the massive devastation they might leave in their wake, driver ants would be way worse if they stuck around in one place. If driver ants infest your house, go stay in a hotel or something for a few days. Just make sure you don't bring any stragglers with you: A NEW *DORYLUS* QUEEN CAN LAY A MILLION EGGS EACH MONTH, SO MAKE SURE YOU DON'T BRING A NEW MAMA ANT TO THE HOTEL BY ACCIDENT.

ACTUAL SIZE!!

RECEPTION

71

WILD BOAR

SCIENTIFIC NAME: *Sus scrofa*

SIZE: 5 ft. (1.5 m) long

WEIGHT: 130 lbs. (59 kg) to 600 lbs. (272 kg)

DIET: Omnivorous

DANGER TO HUMANS: Medium

6 ft.

3 ft.

SCALE TO HUMANS

Full-grown boars will charge enemies with their tusks, intending to gore them.

KNOW YOUR
OPPONENT

(SUS SCROFA)

BOAR JAWS ARE EXTREMELY HARDY: They can crack open hard-shelled nuts, and **even crush bones when scavenging.**

According to Texas A&M University, a wild boar may eat an entire carcass, **"leaving little if any sign behind."**

BOARS ARE VERY HARD-HEADED, with **huge skulls** and powerful necks that enable it to dig in the dirt, snout-first, for food.

NORTH AMERICA

CHINA

➤ WHERE IN THE WORLD?
Wild boars are in all of Eurasia, southern Asia, China, Korea, Japan, the Malay Archipelago, northern Australia and North America.

IN NORTH AMERICA AND AUSTRALIA, wild boars are an invasive species, and hunters make efforts to get rid of them to reduce the threat they pose to native wildlife, domesticated animals, and crops. Worse, pig populations that run free from farms may join up with these wild boars and turn feral, rampaging across the countryside and eating everything in their path.

THE WILD BOAR IS THE ANCESTOR OF THE DOMESTICATED PIG, and it has a fearsome reputation. The boar-hunting implement known as the **boar spear** has a flanged, or rimmed, crosspiece on it—this isn't an additional handhold or a slashing weapon, it's designed to prevent the boar from *impaling itself all the way on the spear* as it makes a final, desperate charge against the hunter. **Boars are curious, smart, and utterly indomitable.**

SURVIVING
A WILD BOAR ATTACK

1 **IN THE WILD, BOARS ARE UNLIKELY TO ATTACK YOU UNLESS** you get between a sow and her piglets, or if you bother a male boar during mating season. Unless you're a boar hunter, the real dangers come from its aftereffects.

COUGH, COUGH.

2 **INFECTING OTHER PIGS.** Wild boars may interact with other domestic animals on their rampages, infecting them with some of the diseases they picked up in the wild. These include bacterial illnesses like brucellosis and viral illnesses like pseudorabies, which aren't necessarily fatal to human beings, but they are to other pigs.

3 **TRICHI-NO-SIR. Be extremely careful about eating boar meat.** Feral pigs and wild boar are vulnerable to parasitic worms. Undercooked boar can carry the *larvae of trichinella roundworms*, leading to a deeply unpleasant illness called trichinosis. All wild meat can be safely cleared of trichinosis risk by **cooking it to an internal temperature of 165 degrees F (74 C).**

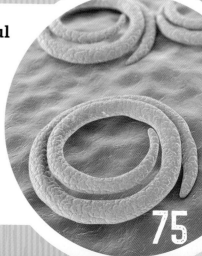

WOLF

SCIENTIFIC NAME: *Canis lupus*

SIZE: 41–63 in. (1–1.6 m) long

WEIGHT: 50–110 lbs. (22.7–50 kg)

DIET: Carnivorous, occasionally supplement their diet with forest plants

DANGER TO HUMANS: Low

6 ft.

3 ft.

SCALE TO HUMANS

OPPONENT (CANIS LUPUS)

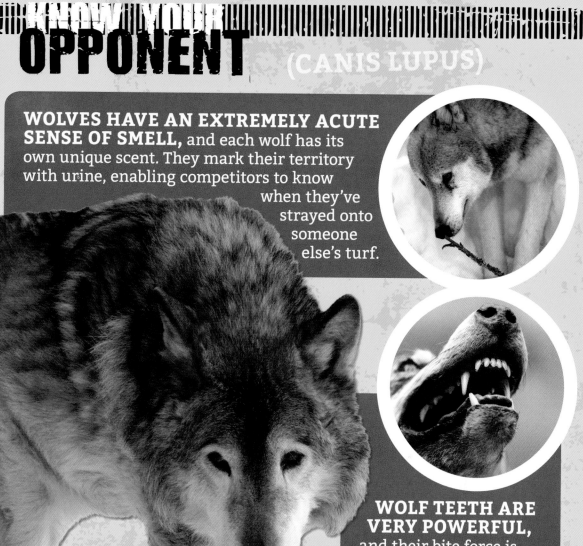

WOLVES HAVE AN EXTREMELY ACUTE SENSE OF SMELL, and each wolf has its own unique scent. They mark their territory with urine, enabling competitors to know when they've strayed onto someone else's turf.

WOLF TEETH ARE VERY POWERFUL, and their bite force is quite strong—about 1500 pounds per square inch. It's strong enough to crush bones.

→ WHERE IN THE WORLD?
Gray wolves are found throughout the entire Northern hemisphere.

77

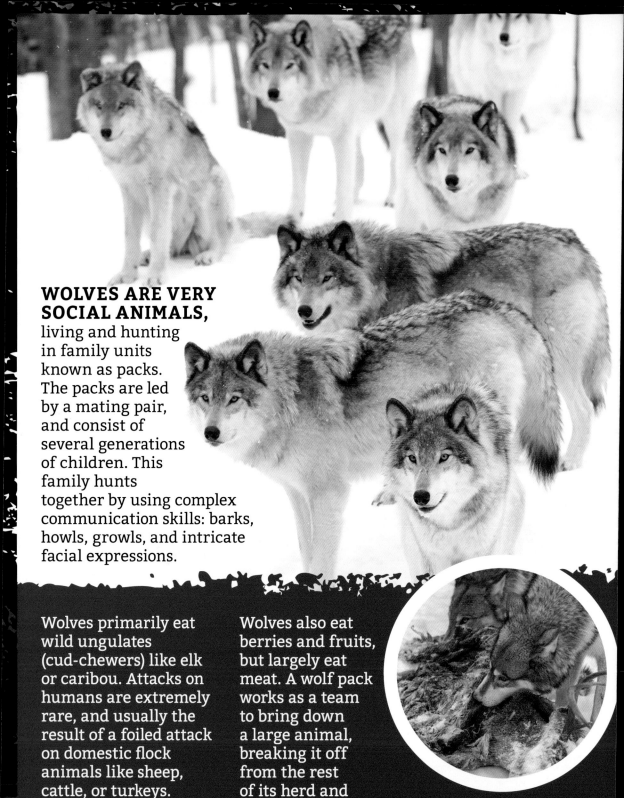

WOLVES ARE VERY SOCIAL ANIMALS, living and hunting in family units known as packs. The packs are led by a mating pair, and consist of several generations of children. This family hunts together by using complex communication skills: barks, howls, growls, and intricate facial expressions.

Wolves primarily eat wild ungulates (cud-chewers) like elk or caribou. Attacks on humans are extremely rare, and usually the result of a foiled attack on domestic flock animals like sheep, cattle, or turkeys.

Wolves also eat berries and fruits, but largely eat meat. A wolf pack works as a team to bring down a large animal, breaking it off from the rest of its herd and cornering it.

SURVIVING
A WOLF ATTACK

AGAIN, WOLVES ARE UNLIKELY TO STALK A HUMAN BEING, BUT IF ON SOME SNOWY NIGHT YOU FIND YOURSELF CORNERED BY A PACK OF WOLVES, HERE'S WHAT YOU GOTTA DO:

1

WHO'S AFRAID OF THE BIG, BAD, WOLF? NOT YOU! You're huge! You're tough! You're full of vinegar! At least, that's what you want the wolf to think. Puff yourself up; make yourself as large and loud as possible. If you have a jacket on, raise it above your head to add height and volume to your profile.

2

DON'T RUN. Wolves are dogs. **DOGS LOVE A CHASE.** These are dogs that tackle and bite at the end of that chase. Besides, you're huge and powerful, remember? You don't need to run from these critters.

3

DON'T MEET THEIR GAZE. It'll look like a territorial challenge. Make a lot of noise and throw stones at them; they'll leave you be.

DO NOT MAKE EYE CONTACT!

MUTE SWANS

SCIENTIFIC NAME: *Cygnus Olor*

SIZE: 55–63 in. (140–160 cm)

WEIGHT: 18.7–32 lbs. (8.5–15 kg)

DIET: Primarily herbivorous

DANGER TO HUMANS: Extremely low

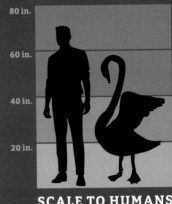

80 in.

60 in.

40 in.

20 in.

SCALE TO HUMANS

A mute swan is one of the heaviest flying birds on the planet.

KNOW YOUR OPPONENT
(CYGNUS OLOR)

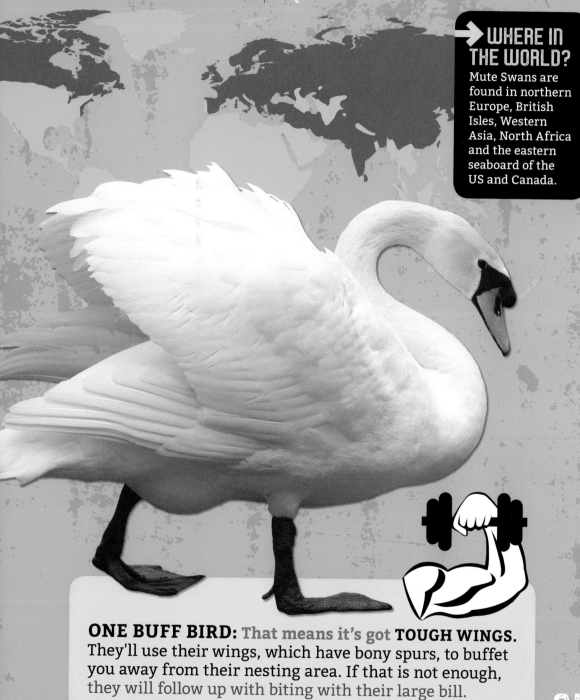

→ WHERE IN THE WORLD?
Mute Swans are found in northern Europe, British Isles, Western Asia, North Africa and the eastern seaboard of the US and Canada.

ONE BUFF BIRD: That means it's got **TOUGH WINGS.** They'll use their wings, which have bony spurs, to buffet you away from their nesting area. If that is not enough, they will follow up with biting with their large bill.

Beautiful and powerful, mute swans are so-called because they don't honk nearly as much as other swans or geese. They do make noises, however, especially hisses to demonstrate territorial anger.

SWANS PRIMARILY EAT AQUATIC VEGETATION. Their long necks allow them to feed from the riverbed. Male mute swans are extremely territorial, too, which makes shooing away a swan family very difficult.

SURVIVING
A SWAN ATTACK

MUTE SWANS ARE DEFENSIVE, NOT AGGRESSIVE. IT'S UNLIKELY THAT A SWAN WILL EVER SEEK OUT A CONFRONTATION WITH A HUMAN UNLESS YOU APPROACH A NESTING SWAN. IF YOU STUMBLE ONTO ONE BY ACCIDENT WHEN BOATING OR KAYAKING, EXERCISE CAUTION. YOU DON'T WANT TO END UP IN THE PATH OF A NESTING MUTE SWAN.

HISS!!!

1 LISTEN FOR THE HISS.
An agitated mute swan will ruffle its feathers and hiss angrily if you're bothering it.

2 MOVE AWAY.
The end goal of a swan attack is for you to leave the area. It doesn't want to kill you; it just wants you to go away.

NOT WELCOME

FLYING SNAKES

SCIENTIFIC NAME: Genus *Chrysopelea*

SIZE: 2–4 ft. (.6–1.2 m)

WEIGHT: 16–35 oz. (450 g–1 kg)

DIET: Carnivorous

DANGER TO HUMANS: Extremely low

6 ft.

3 ft.

SCALE TO HUMANS

Flying snakes are members of the *Colubridae* family, which means their venom-fangs are located toward the rear of their mouths.

KNOW YOUR OPPONENT (CHRYSOPELEA)

Flying snakes can flatten their bodies and expand their ribs to create a kind of simple "wing," enabling them to glide (or at least fall gracefully) through the treetops.

SOUTHEAST ASIA

→ WHERE IN THE WORLD?
Flying snakes are found in Southeast Asia, the Malay Archipelago, and the Philippines.

FLYING SNAKES ARE BEAUTIFUL, WEIRDLY ELEGANT CREATURES that launch themselves from treetop to treetop, chasing small mammals and reptiles. They go after bats and other creatures that can escape from tree to tree, and have evolved this gliding strategy: it uses special muscles to flatten its body, and then "swims" through the air in a slithering motion.

It's venomous, but not venomous enough to hurt or kill a human being. It uses its venom primarily to incapacitate bats, rodents, lizards, and birds.

SURVIVING
A FLYING SNAKE ATTACK

THE IDEA OF A VENOMOUS SNAKE DROPPING DOZENS OF FEET FROM THE TREETOPS DOES SOUND TERRIFYING. BUT WE'RE FORTUNATE THAT THE FLYING SNAKE ISN'T AFTER HUMANS.

THEY'RE PRETTY SMALL, AS FAR AS SNAKES GO, AND AREN'T INTERESTED IN DEFENDING TERRITORY. Some have even been captured for the exotic pet trade, and while they don't attack their owners, they don't much like captivity, and soon get sick and die. **Really, there should be a book for flying snakes called:**

WHEN HUMANS ATTACK:
A FLYING SNAKE'S GUIDE TO SURVIVAL

TSETSE FLY

SCIENTIFIC NAME: Genus *glossina*

SIZE: .2–.6 in. (.5 – 1.5 cm)

WEIGHT: Too small to measure

DIET: Mammalian blood

DANGER TO HUMANS: High

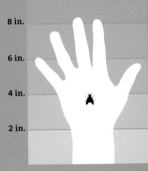

8 in.

6 in.

4 in.

2 in.

SCALE TO HUMANS

THIS TUBE-LIKE STRUCTURE IS CALLED THE PROBOSCIS; it's the mouth-like organ that tsetses use to **suck blood.**

KNOW YOUR OPPONENT

(GENUS GLOSSINA)

THE PROBOSCIS **is tipped with rasps and teeth to saw through flesh**, digging into a wound. Blood wells up and mixes with fly saliva, and then gets pumped up the proboscis into the fly's gut. Pay attention to the saliva step; it'll be important in a minute.

AFRICA

➡ WHERE IN THE WORLD? Tsetse flies are found in sub-saharan Africa.

TSETSE FLIES HAVE A DISTINCTIVE WING ARRANGEMENT; when they're at rest, they fold directly on top of one another.

TSETSE IS THE TSWANA WORD FOR FLY, SO REALLY, TSETSE FLY IS REDUNDANT.

This little bloodsucking bug is responsible for the spread of terrible illness throughout sub-Saharan Africa, in the form of sleeping sickness (a fatal-if-untreated disease that affects humans) and rinderpest (a viral epidemic that slaughtered cattle and other mammals). It's not the fly itself that's immediately responsible so much as it is the many parasites and fellow-traveler germs that hitch rides inside these large beasties.

Sleeping sickness is a parasitic disease that affects the brain, disrupting the sleep schedule and causing drowsiness in the day and wakefulness at night. Eventually, the illness leads to seizures, psychosis, and death. **IT'S REALLY, REALLY BAD.**

There are up to 10,000 cases of West African sleeping sickness reported each year, however, it is unknown how many cases go unreported.

SURVIVING
A TSETSE ATTACK

1

TRAP 'EM. Brightly-colored traps treated with insecticides are effective in attracting and killing small populations of tsetses, but in order to be truly effective, they need to be applied on a massive scale.

2

POUR IT ON. Pouring bug repellent on cattle, covering their backs, stomachs and legs, is known to the World Health Organization as an effective strategy to prevent fly-borne diseases from spreading from cattle to humans, and from preventing those illnesses in cattle in the first place.

3

ZAP 'EM. THE STERILE INSECT TECHNIQUE. Male tsetse flies are raised in laboratories and sterilized with radiation; then they are released into the wild to mate. No eggs get fertilized, and tsetse populations drop quickly as a result. This is the most expensive and labor-intensive form of tsetse control, but scientists are always working on ways to improve and simplify this method.

PEREGRINE FALCON

SCIENTIFIC NAME: *Falco peregrinus*

SIZE: 2.2–3.9 ft. (0.7–1.2 m) wingspan

WEIGHT: 1.5–3.5 lbs. (.7–1.6 kg)

DIET: Carnivorous

DANGER TO HUMANS: Low

6 ft.

3 ft.

SCALE TO HUMANS

The peregrine falcon is the fastest animal on the planet.

KNOW YOUR OPPONENT

(FALCO PEREGRINUS)

IF THE FALCON'S PUNCH DOESN'T DO IT, THE NOTCHED BEAK WILL. That little nub on the upper beak increases the cracking force of its bite, **making it easier to snap the spines of prey animals.**

THIS IS THE KILLING BLOW, RIGHT HERE.

It's not the talons that do the killing, it's the whole foot. **When peregrines enter their dive, they hit their prey mid-air with the foot balled-up, almost like a fist.** At this tremendous speed, the force of the blow stuns or kills the prey outright. Then the falcon catches and carries off its prize.

➡ WHERE IN THE WORLD?

Peregrine falcons can be found worldwide—from tundra to deserts.

In its hunting dives, the peregrine falcon can reach speeds over 200 miles per hour (322 kph), striking its prey like a living guided missile.

Peregrine falcons are migratory, covering vast distances in their lifetimes, which gave rise to their name. **Peregrine is another word for a pilgrim or a wanderer.**

Peregrine falcons mostly eat other birds and have extended their reach from environments as diverse as the Arctic Circle all the way to high-rise buildings in big cities.

SURVIVING
A FALCON ATTACK

FALCONS DON'T TEND TO ATTACK PEOPLE; INSTEAD, HUMANS HAVE TRAINED FALCONS TO HUNT FOR THEM IN A KIND OF SEMI-TAME RELATIONSHIP CALLED FALCONRY.

In 2013, conservationists at the University of Toledo in Ohio temporarily removed some falcon chicks from the rooftop of a clock tower to check them for exposure to pesticides, attach tracking bands, and take blood samples. **The parental peregrines were not happy, and dive-bombed the researchers** (not from a full hunting dive), attacking with their claws. **The researchers came prepared, wearing solid safety helmets and carrying medieval-style wooden shields.** These were enough to repel the falcons long enough to take the samples and return the chicks to their nest. **FORTUNATELY, NO HUMANS OR CHICKS WERE HARMED.**

95

CONCLUSION A.K.A. THE END

WE HOPE THIS BOOK HELPS YOU BE MORE AWARE OF THE POTENTIAL DANGERS OUT THERE AS YOU EXPLORE YOUR WORLD.

That said, the lesson we hope to convey in this book most of all is this: don't bother wild animals. Most of the time, the creatures listed in this book will not harm you unless you antagonize them. Don't go looking for trouble, and, more than likely, trouble won't go looking for you.

Ours is a world in delicate balance—some of the animals detailed are quite endangered in the wild, whether through poaching or habitat destruction. They have far more to fear from us as human beings than we do from them.

But sometimes they forget that, and that's when this book comes in handy.

TO RECAP:
STAY SAFE OUT THERE!

1 GO FOR THE EYES.

2 PROTECT YOUR ORGANS.

3 DON'T TOUCH THE BRIGHTLY-COLORED CRITTERS.